Growing Up in God's Image

A New Approach to the Facts of Life Talk

What to Say and How to Say it

By Carolyn J. Smith

Growing Up in God's Image
Copyright 2012 Carolyn J. Smith
Published by Full Quiver Publishing
PO Box 244
Pakenham, Ontario
K0A 2X0

ISBN Number: 978-0-9736736-4-7
Printed and bound in USA

Cover design by Carolyn and Jim Smith
and James Hrkach
Illustrations by James Hrkach

NATIONAL LIBRARY OF CANADA CATALOGUING IN
PUBLICATION

Smith, Carolyn J.
Growing in God's Image
Edited by Ellen Gable Hrkach

The roses on the front cover honor St. Thérèse of the Little Flower to whom I prayed for intercession. She sought holiness through the little things of each day. She grew in a child-like spirituality that began in her family life and is an inspiration to us all. It was her road to sainthood.

She is also the patron saint of missionaries because she united her daily prayers and sacrifices with the work of the missions. I believe that family life and sexuality can be considered a modern missionary field.

St. Thérèse, pray for us.

I would like to dedicate this book to all families. How different would our families be if we could but grasp even a small measure of the wonder and awe with which God created us? *"Let Us make man in Our image, after Our likeness;"* (Gen. 1:26)

We are His image to our world. We live and grow "through Him, with Him, and in Him in the unity of the Holy Spirit." As the Center of every family, His love will bind us, sustain us, protect us, and guide us.
"Glory be to the Father and to the Son and to the Holy Spirit. As it was in the beginning is now and ever shall be world without end. Amen."

Carolyn Smith

Table of Contents

Dear Parents,

You may wonder at what age is it appropriate to talk to children about the facts of reproduction. Keep in mind that there is never just one talk. It is rather a process that is very ongoing both by word and by example.

As a suggestion: in our family, we begin talking about the fact that we are created in the image and likeness of God when the children are very young and first learn about creation. To help them understand more about how we image God, the ideas covered on pages 13 through 16 can be taught as early as kindergarten and reinforced throughout the years to follow. Likewise, modesty (p. 18) is about more than just clothing; it teaches respect for self and for others and it begins with the very young. I begin to use this material more formally with my children toward the end of the fifth grade. By this time, their bodies have begun to change and they are asking serious questions. (Some, especially boys, may not be ready until the sixth grade, or even the seventh grade.)

I have also used this material differently with my children depending on the developmental stage of each one and depending on the influences of each one's particular environment. For instance, with some I went only as far as explaining the changes taking place within the body, and saved the discussion about inter-course for the following year or even later. With some, I covered both discussions in the same sitting.

I have found that age thirteen or fourteen is a very good time to review it and go into further considerations, (i.e., topics covered in the "Thoughts to Consider"). One way is to give the book to them to reread on their own and then discuss any questions they might have. I then discuss additional "Thoughts to Consider" when they reach dating age. And, I give them this book as a gift when they are beyond high school age and on their own. I have also shared it with other college students and young married couples who said it opened up for them a whole new world of understanding and appreciation.

You know each of your children best. You know the circumstances of your family and community. These considerations enter into your decision to begin using this material with your children. By first reading it yourself, you may find that it enhances your own appreciation and understanding of sacramental marriage in preparation for planned as well as impromptu discussions with your children. Feedback has told me that this book can be of help to you and your family at all ages.

Sincerely,

Carolyn Smith

Carolyn Smith

INTRODUCTION

"To each individual the manifestation of the Spirit is given for some benefit."
(1 Corinthians 12:7)

It's been many years since that first talk with my oldest daughter about the facts of life, but I remember it very well. Like most moms, I was a bit nervous and consternated over what to say. Actually, I remember resenting that I had to talk with her so soon. I felt pressured because many of the children at school were already "knowledgeable." Hearing something from a classmate was the last thing I wanted to happen. I didn't want her to hear about "sex." I wanted her to hear about the beauty of God's gift of love. I was getting ready to tell her about a very special and holy love, the love that existed between her father and me. My husband, Jim, is truly God's gift to me. So I went to the Source of the gift and asked Him, "Lord, what do you want me to say to her?"

I felt certain God wanted me to start at the beginning with Him. After all, He *is Love* itself. *All* love, especially this love, comes from Him. God created us to love Him and to love each other; therefore we should talk about His creation of Adam and Eve and His plan for marriage from the very beginning. What we have today is nothing new. It has existed since the beginning of time. And, in the One that we *image*, it has always existed! Thus, this theme became the beginning of the "facts of life" talk.

The second theme came to me many years later while away with my husband for a weekend. The gift came during Mass between the consecration and the communion. After Mass, I couldn't wait to tell Jim! It left me absolutely in *awe* that God has given to married people a love that resembles His own in the Eucharist!

I was then able to share this with my fifth daughter, (and the sixth, seventh, and eighth) when I talked to her about the "facts of life." Her reaction was everything a mom could hope for. She looked up at me and said in wonder, "Wow, **THAT** is really neat!"

The third theme talks about marriage as a sacrament. What God intended from the very beginning of creation was elevated to a new level of sanctity by His Son. God is intimately present to every couple through the sacrament. He is the very Center of their life and love.

The first time I was inclined to share all of this came after a call from a friend. In the course of the conversation, she mentioned that it was time to talk to her oldest daughter. She had tied herself up in knots wondering what to say. I told her that I'd done it five times already and would be glad to share with her what I do, if she wished. So we set a time and she came to my house -- very nervous. But, what a thrill it was for me to watch her leave a little while later, not only at peace, but excited and anxious to talk with her daughter.

She called me later to tell me that it went great. But, she wanted more. She told me that I should and must write it down in a way that would help lots of people, just like it helped her. She said that there is such a need for this, especially in today's world. (The 'funny' thing was that my husband had also strongly suggested the same thing several times already, including that very morning. The Spirit can be such a "pest!")

So, my purpose is exactly that -- to help! And, if it helps you, thank the Holy Spirit! It is His gift to us all!

In addition, my husband, Jim, very generously contributed the section, "Talking With Your Son," for fathers to use based on what he covered with our sons.

There is no doubt in my mind that God has willed this. He wants parents to sit with their children and tell them about *love*. He has entrusted our children, His children, to **us**, not to the schools, and certainly, not to the state. There are others, such as pastors and teachers, who can lend a valuable hand when needed. They give assistance when we ask for it, but they can never take our place.

We need to be reminded and our children need to hear that *nothing* on this earth is separate from God. When somebody draws a picture or writes a story, we see a part of that person in their work. This is most true of God. He is the *Author of it all* and so we see a part of Him in every form of creation. Because He created human beings above all the rest and actually made us in His likeness, He should be the most visible in us! Just as He once did, He still comes into our world through the family.

You will find that as you and your children use this book together, you will be seeing God's plan for each of us as male and female and God's plan for marriage and family just as he intended from the very beginning of creation. You will see it as sacramental and holy, an image of God Himself and a reflection of His love for us. In very simple words, this is the message John Paul II conveyed in his *Theology of the Body*. Of paramount importance to his papacy was that all of God's people answer the universal call to holiness, especially through their vocations in life. Most of us are called to the married life, but all of us depend on the sacrament of matrimony for our very existence and formation. If we want holy men and women serving God in this world according to His purpose, we must begin with holy families.

In our world, the meaning of family and its value in society has been lost. I pray for its conversion.

Author's Note

Blessed John Paul II's *Theology of the Body* has been widely circulated and appreciated by adults and, more recently, by teens. By using this book with your younger children, you will be introducing them even earlier to a very simple and practical interpretation of this inspired truth about the human way of life and love as intended from the hands of our Creator. In reading the following pages, some have remarked that what is written here is very idealistic. My response to that is, "Yes, I agree." Like John Paul II's *Theology of the Body*, it is indeed idealistic. In fact, everything Christ taught us is idealistic. How many of us keep the Ten Commandments daily? More importantly, how many of us live Christ's command to "Love one another as I have loved you"? Do we live the Two Greatest Commandments? Do we live the Eight Beatitudes all the time? Do we practice the Corporal and Spiritual Works of Mercy perfectly? The answer to all of these questions is an obvious, "No."

Does that mean that it is unattainable? By ourselves, it is certainly unattainable, and God never expected that. That is why He gave us the sacraments and His tremendous gift of grace, a share in His divine life. He told us to come to Him constantly in prayer. "What you ask in my name shall be given to you." "Knock and the door will be opened." He has a plan for the world and He has a plan for each of us within the greater plan. We must put ourselves in His arms just as our infants put themselves in ours; total dependence. With His help, we can live in His image. We'll fall, but we'll get back up again, just as He did. We can do it with God's help. We would be foolish to try it alone.

So, my belief is that in this very first presentation, we give our children God's way, pure and untouched. Then, we teach our kids to strive to be their best, with God's help!

Carolyn Smith

I. SPOUSAL LOVE REFLECTS THE LOVE OF THE TRINITY

We are going to talk about the kind of love that makes us a family. When we talk about love, we always begin with God, Who is Love Itself. God Himself is a Family bound by Love.

Image and Likeness

> *"Let us make man in our image, after our likeness.*
> *God created man in his image;*
> *in the divine image he created him;*
> *male and female he created them."*
>
> (Gen. 1:26-27)

Then, God blessed them. He first created the man and then He said:

> *"It is not good for the man to be alone. I will make a suitable*
> *partner for him. ...So the Lord God cast a deep sleep on the man,*
> *and while he was asleep, he took out one of the ribs and closed up its*
> *place with flesh. The Lord God then built up into a woman the rib*
> *that he had taken from the man. When he brought her to the man,*
> *the man said:*
>
> > *'This one, at last, is bone off my bones*
> > *And flesh of my flesh;*
> > *This one shall be called 'woman,'*
> > *For out of 'her man' this one has been taken.'*
>
> *This is why a man leaves his father and mother and clings to his*
> *wife and the two become one body."* (Gen. 2:18, 21-24)

God saw that the man needed a companion, someone to love and to share life. God loved them so much that, at the very start of creation, He gave them to each other in marriage. It was His gift to Adam and Eve and all of humanity. Because He made them in His image, their love would also be an image of His love.

The Blessed Trinity, Who is God and *love* itself, is the source of all love. God and His love for us is a great mystery. That is why it is so hard for us to describe what true love really is. Christ tells us that our love should reflect His love and He asks us to *"love one another as I have loved you."* What is He asking of us? His love for us meant giving up His life. Our love is therefore going to mean giving up of ourselves for the good of others. Christ invites us to **live the mystery of love with Him as His companion.** He knows that He is asking something that is impossible for us on our own; it is possible only with Him as our constant Companion and Guide. **With the reassurance of His presence, grace, and love, He asks us to accept His invitation to live this mystery of love for a lifetime and longer.**

This great mystery is truly a gift from God. He created us with a soul that, like Him, has the power to know and to choose, and therefore, to love. God, Who has an infinite knowledge of all creation, chooses to infinitely love all He has made. To love as God loves, we must grow in knowledge of Him and creation, because it is in Him alone that we find *true love* and in His creation that we find the expression of it. Then we can begin to love as He loves, while remaining patient with the limits of our human nature. This is the mystery that God has given us as a gift to enjoy for a lifetime and longer!

God created us in His image and likeness. Just as children resemble their human parents, we, as God's children resemble Him.
God is: All-knowing
     All-loving
     All-fruitful.

His love flows from all that He knows about us. His love is a free gift of Self -- no strings attached. He *knows* us better than we know ourselves. He knows the absolute truth of who we are and He *chooses* to infinitely *love* us. There are no limits to His giving. There are no limits to the life that He shares. There are no limits to His goodness. The fruits of His love are endless.

God made us to: Know
     Love
     Be fruitful.

Our love for God grows as we grow in knowledge of Him. Our love for another person also grows as we grow in knowledge of that person. Our love should be a free gift of self -- no strings attached. (Two people meet and become acquainted with each other. They begin to know each other and become friends. They get to know each other better and begin to love. They grow in that knowledge of one another and learn that they seek the same things in life. They want to share life together, so they commit to love each other in marriage. Love is a *choice* based on all that they *know* about each another.) When we love in this way, it is always fruitful because we are imitating God's love. In doing this we help strengthen the Body of Christ alive in this world. Our love, then, is life-giving. God created each one of us to know, love, and serve Him in this world in the same way that His own Son came to know, love, and serve. We are called to imitate His goodness; to imitate his gift of self.

This means that we are called to be His instruments in the world. In a very awesome way, mothers and fathers are called to be co-creators with God. They are cooperators with God in bringing His children into the world, and thus, adding to His family. Mom and Dad supply the physical part, and God creates the soul, which will live forever.

Family Love Resembles God's Love

As family we are created in the image and likeness of God. "Let **Us** make man in **Our** image, after **Our** likeness." (Gen. 1:26)

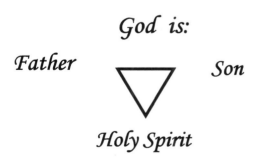

God is:

Father   *Son*

Holy Spirit

The Holy Spirit is the sign of the love between the Father and the Son. The Father and the Son sent the Holy Spirit into the world full of Their love to help others love more fully. God's work of bringing us home to Him can only be accomplished with the help of the Holy Spirit.

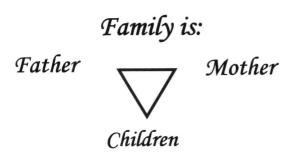

Family is:

Father   *Mother*

Children

The children are the sign of the love between father and mother. Father and mother send their children into the world nourished by their love to serve others. By relying on the Holy Spirit, father, mother, and children accomplish God's work in the world and are His instruments in helping others to love more fully. This family love extended toward others images the Trinity as well; God, family, and others. Our families are the first instruments of God's plan.

Father, Son, and Holy Spirit are family, a community of Persons. They cannot be separated because their bond of love is so strong that it makes them One God, one Family. No One can live without the other Two. They give continuous love to one another. They share all things. Each One has a separate role, but All live for the same purpose. This Family of Persons is the reason the world exists, the reason the world is redeemed, and the reason it is sanctified. Their mission is to share their kingdom with as many of us as possible.

Family is the nucleus for the world community. Although families can tragically separate, and sadly, at times necessarily so, the family's spiritual, biological and psychological bonds still remain. All families need to draw on the grace of God to sustain them. God made family to be the source of strength in the world. God's work in the world depends on the strength and holiness of its families.

Father and mother are the first lesson in love for their children. With God as the Center of their marriage and family, their love grows in reflection of God's love. Continuously nurtured by His grace through prayer and the sacraments, they grow in love for one another and for their children. In turn, their children are called to respond in love for their parents and for one another. Each member of the family expresses love in willingness to give and share. Each member of the family has a separate role, but all live for the same purpose. Using their God-given talents in image of the Trinity, they give to each other and to others in order to build up the kingdom of God with as many of us as possible, for we are all called to holiness! We are not truly home until we are home with God.

Respect for Our Bodies

(The following will guide you in speaking with your child about respect and care for his/her body, especially during puberty and the years following. One way to approach this section is to read it together and talk about it together. Begin by explaining to your child: "Your body will soon be changing and maturing.")

God created us holy like Himself. The lesson here is on the sacredness of the body. He didn't create only a part of us "holy" and another part "human." He created body and soul as one. They separate only at death. The body is actually the outward expression of what is in the soul. He created us as sacred beings -- images of Himself -- and placed us over all the other creatures. When He was finished, He called it good.

In Baptism, He makes His home within our soul and dwells in the tabernacles of our bodies. When He comes to us in the Eucharist, He makes His home within each of our bodies in a very real and physical way. For this reason, as well as for the individual purposes for which He created each one of us, it is very important that we take good care of our bodies. To do God's work in the world, we need strength of body, mind, and soul. Remember that Jesus Himself used His human body to carry out the work of redemption. He used His human hands to heal, his human mouth to teach and console, his human ears to listen, and his human feet to visit the sick and even just to visit friends. Through his humanity He showed us His divinity. In the same way, we should be the face of God to others. Mary, too, used her body to cooperate in the work of redemption. After all, it was through her body that Jesus came into the world. Therefore, because our bodies house God and because we need healthy bodies to do His work, we:

- take regular baths or showers
- wash before eating meals
- eat the proper foods for good nutrition
- see the doctor for check-ups and when otherwise necessary
- get proper rest
- exercise body and mind regularly
- dress in clean clothes according to the weather
- dress modestly to avoid unnecessary temptation and to
- guard purity

Modesty refers to the value we put on our own privacy as well as the respect we show for the privacy of others. A modest person recognizes the value of his or her own privacy and does not surrender it for casual reasons. A modest person respects another person's space, whether it be property, personal belongings, thoughts, feelings, etc. It means recognizing the true human dignity of each person in body and soul. Modesty is about respect for ourselves and respect for others.

This begins at an early age with learning to respect what is mine and what is yours. As we begin to grow up, we close bedroom and bathroom doors. We knock before entering out of respect for another's privacy. We recognize personal space such as dresser drawers, closets, desks, mail, purses, etc.

When we begin to play with other children, we also begin to make decisions on our own. We learn to share ideas and to respect the ideas of another person. We learn to respect another's feelings and worth. We make friends and want to share what is ours. We begin to distinguish between what is OK and what is *not* OK to share. With help from Mom and Dad, this also begins with the very young. For example, they may not want to share toys, but on the other hand, they may want to share their food and/or drink. In the same way, it would be unjust to share details of a family quarrel, which is something private to the family. This is gossiping. When we gossip about anyone, we hurt others as well as ourselves by sharing inappropriate information, whether it is true or untrue. We are guilty of damaging another's good name, which cannot be repaired so simply as a broken window. We are also guilty of leading others to gossip and do further damage. Our conversations should always make us better people. Our conversations should always make our friends better people.

We learn to respect another's private conversation, whether in the same room or on the phone, and to distance ourselves from it. When someone confides in us, we must keep it private. To do otherwise would be a betrayal of trust and a show of disrespect for the privacy and dignity of that person.

Modesty necessarily refers, then, to the protection of body *and* soul. Children and young people must learn to respect the body itself as a gift from God, a temple of the Holy Spirit, and a part of Christ's Mystical Body in Whom we live. Frequent reception of the sacraments of Penance and Holy Eucharist is an invaluable means of guarding the purity of body and soul.

Modesty demands that we protect those private and sacred parts of the body, i.e., those parts we refer to as the sexual parts of the body; those parts that make us male and female (those parts that we cover with a bathing suit). Here, too, it is important to know what is OK and what is not OK to share with the eyes and ears of others.

The eyes are the windows of the soul. It is important to guard the senses to protect the soul. Consider the many things in our world that appeal so strongly to the senses and influence thought and behavior: television, movies, clothing fashions, books, music, and much more. All can be instruments that help us become better individuals. They can also be instruments that degrade the human person, especially the sexuality of the human person.

God's gift of sexuality is intended for noble and holy purposes. God specifically makes the sexual organs for expressing devotion between husband and wife -- a devotion God uses for bringing new life into the world and for nurturing that new life. So, they are called the reproductive organs or genitals or genitalia (a derivative of the Latin word, *genitus*, the past participle of *gingere*, meaning "to beget" or "to give birth"). Their use, therefore, is reserved for the Sacrament of Matrimony.

In marriage, husband and wife will give totally to each other in love. They will give themselves to each other before God, thereby helping each other and their children to one day become saints in heaven. They will give themselves:

- **Spiritually**, through prayer, sacrifice, and support of the faith.
- **Emotionally**, in all their joys and sorrows, in their good times and bad times, as well as in the daily routines of life.
- **Mentally**, through the thoughts, ideas, and goals that they share.
- **Physically**, through a special gift of love that God gives them to deepen their love and to bring children into the world.

We begin early, during the time of *puberty*, to get ready for all these things. It is part of the process of growing up. (Can mention here the maturation that has already taken place since birth. Be sure to talk about growth of the entire person, i.e., physical, emotional, mental, and spiritual growth.) Sometime between the ages of 9 and 13, young girls and boys begin to notice that the sexual parts of the body are changing.

Author's Note: When talking to your children about changes in the body, mothers should be with their daughters, and fathers with their sons. There are exceptions to this, of course, but this is the norm. Following are two sections: one for mothers and daughters and one for fathers and sons. My husband and I tried to provide the "script" for you to make it easy. (Many parents have told me that having the words right in front of them is a terrific help.) There are also very simple but clear diagrams in the back of the book. Some parents like to use them. Others prefer not to use them. Therefore, I placed them at the back to use at your discretion.

How To Talk With Your Daughter

(The words in italics are provided for you to talk with our daughter about changes taking place or about to take place in her body. The purpose here is not an in-depth biology lesson. Rather, it is to help your daughter understand that she is growing in mind, body, and soul. She will soon take on a more womanly appearance, but becoming a woman is a gradual process that involves the whole person. God is good. He doesn't expect us to do it all at once.)

1. Physical Growth

Someday, if you become a mother, your breasts will contain the milk that feeds your baby. You may have already noticed your breasts changing. This means that you are beginning to **mature**. *You are becoming a young woman and your body will now slowly begin to take the shape of an adult woman. It may be time to buy your first bra, (or perhaps that has already happened). This first bra will be fine for awhile, but in about a year, (maybe sooner, maybe later), you will outgrow this one. You need to let mom know so that she can fit you properly in the next size.*

You may have noticed another sign of your body changing, i.e., the appearance of hair on the pubic area. It will start out scarce and will eventually cover the area. It won't grow like the hair on your head. It will remain short and curly.

You may also have noticed changes in the oils of your skin and hair. These changes may necessitate a daily bath or shower and the use of a deodorant to prevent body odor. You may also find that you need to shampoo more frequently to prevent your hair from becoming too oily.

2. Monthly Cycle

There is another part of growing up that you will notice some time from now. It is called **menstruation**. *Sometimes we refer to it as a period or a monthly cycle. (The word, menses, means month.) The process of menstruation begins inside your body in your reproductive organs. God is slowly preparing your body to become an adult woman. If He has chosen you for physical motherhood someday, this is part of the process that will make that possible. (It will take many years for your body, mind, and soul to mature. If you haven't already, it is a good time to begin the daily habit of praying for wisdom to know the vocation God has chosen for you. He created you a uniquely feminine person to accomplish a particular role in building His Kingdom.)*

By looking at the illustration of the reproductive system, we can understand how it works.

Ovary and Ova
Fallopian Tubes   *See Diagram A, page 65, which shows the*
Uterus   *female reproductive organs. It will help your*
Cervix   *daughter see what she looks like on the inside.*
Vagina

Now, go to Diagram B, page 67, of a monthly cycle that shows the path of an egg and follow it along with your daughter:

> *Inside each ovary are ova, or tiny eggs. Each month, (or approximately every 28 days) one egg breaks through from the ovary and enters the fallopian tube. (Typically, this will happen on one side one month, and then on the other side the next month. In other words, the process will alternate sides each month.) It then begins to travel down the tube. As it travels, notice that the lining of the uterus begins to build itself up with blood and fluid. It does this in case the egg is fertilized. The fertilized egg is a baby and will need a soft, warm place to nestle. This is where the baby will find the nourishment necessary to grow and develop inside of the mother.*

> *During this time, as the egg is making its way down the fallopian tube, the lining of the uterus continues to build itself up with rich blood and fluid. Approximately 24 hours after ovulation, the ovum or egg dissipates.*

*If the egg has **not** been fertilized, there is no need for this nice rich lining. The egg dies and the lining of blood and fluid sloughs off and leaves the body through the vagina. This flow of blood is slow and gradual and usually takes about 5 days. However, this might not be the case in the beginning.*

*In the very beginning, you might notice just a tiny spot of blood on your underwear. It might be red, but brown is also a possibility. You might then notice some more "spotting." This would be the beginning of your first "period" and it will probably have a light flow, but **everyone is different**. Normally, the flow on the first 2 days is a little heavier and then, the flow on the final 3 days becomes lighter with each day. If your period should last less than 5 days or more than 5 days, it is perfectly normal. Remember, **everyone is different**! Your first periods may or may not be a month apart. It sometimes takes time for the body to adjust. You might have a period and then get another the next month. Or, you might not get another period for 2 months or even 3 months. This is something you just won't know until it happens.*

Even when it gets established, the length of each cycle will also vary from person to person. These things you will know better when the time comes.

3. Sanitary Considerations

Now, it is time to bring out all the "paraphernalia"--- tampons, pads, and panty liners -- for the heavy days and for the light days. (Your daughter will want to know how she can care for herself. The frontal diagram A, page 65 will help you explain about tampons. Use a panty to demonstrate how a pad is worn.)

These tampons and/or pads will catch the flow of blood from your body. On the first 2 days, you should use tampons or pads made for heavier flow. You will need to change them every 3-4 hours. On the other days, you can use tampons or pads made for the lighter days. Again, you should change them every 3-4 hours. (Because everyone is different, you may sometimes need to change more often.)

If you choose to wear a tampon, it is a good idea to back it up with a pad or panty liner to avoid embarrassments. Because you won't always know the exact day that your period will start, it is a good idea to carry a pad or tampon in your purse. If you do get "caught," there are dispensers in all public restrooms for women.

(Note to parent: At some future time, you may want to teach your daughter some aspects of NFP such as recording her temperature and/or mucus observations. If a girl is charting her signs and symptoms of fertility, it is unusual to get "caught" because she more accurately knows the first day of her next period. Additionally, regarding tampons: although rare, tampons can cause Toxic Shock Syndrome in some women. Remember to change frequently according to the directions on the box and let Mom know whether you notice any burning or itching.)

Remember that menstruation happens in every woman who has ever lived. This is what makes it physically possible for women to become mothers.

4. Hormones

*A word about **hormones**: Hormones are substances in the body that make all of this work. Different hormones are present to a greater or lesser degree at different times of the cycle. There are several different types of hormones and they are of vital importance to the body, especially to the reproductive system. These are the hormones that make you female.*

*These same hormones can sometimes affect our emotions. Especially when you're just beginning to grow up, you may feel like your emotions have gone "hay-wire." Or, you may wonder, **"Why do I feel like this?"** (For example, you may feel "weepy" or "on-edge" for no* *apparent reason.)   Don't worry! It could very possibly be your hormones working over-time. If this happens, try to be patient with yourself and your body. If you can recognize what it is, it can help both you and those around you.*

5. Male Biology

(Note: It is helpful for girls to understand a little bit about the male biology and that boys also experience changes in their bodies.)

*As with the female body, the male body has its reproductive organs which begin to function at puberty. For the most part the male sexual organs are on the outside the body. As depicted in Diagram C, page 69, the most apparent male sex organ is the **penis**, which is located in front of the **scrotum**, a sac of loose skin that contains **testicles**.*

*The testicles produce the male hormone testosterone, which causes the various physical changes in the male body as it transitions through puberty. The physical changes that occur are a deepening of the voice, facial and pubic hair, and enlargement of the penis, scrotum, and testicles. The testicles, **testes**, produce **sperm**, the male reproductive cell which fertilizes the egg (ovum) in the female.*

*The sperm leave the testicles though a small tube called the **vas deferens**. Sperm is carried in milky fluid called **semen** and passed through the **urethra**. Urine also passes through the urethra, but it never passes through the penis at the same time.*

*When a young man reaches puberty he may experience involuntary ejaculations at night when he is sleeping. An **ejaculation** is a discharge of semen in short abrupt spurts. These so-called "wet dreams" are a normal occurrence during adolescence and are sometimes associated with stimulating dreams.*

*Male **hormones**, like the female hormones in girls, are the substances that make all this happen. They do not have the same cyclical nature as the girls, but might have similar physical and emotional affects because they are not quite established yet.*

For example, a boy may experience his voice cracking, fluctuating between high and low tones, before it establishes itself at a deeper level. This may cause some embarrassment and/or awkwardness requiring patience and understanding from both self and others. Emotional ups and downs can be felt in other ways as well and may even seem uncontrollable at times. Knowing the reason for it can certainly be helpful.

6. Growth is Gradual

There is so much to growing up and so much to look forward to in the process. Thank God that He stretches it out for us by not asking us to grow up all at one time. It's important to enjoy where you are at each age and not try to rush it, because you will never be that age again. You know that growing up won't always be easy, but nothing very worthwhile in life is easy. It is a wonderful and challenging time -- and, of course, it goes on forever, because we never stop growing up!

This is a continuing process of maturing into the man or woman God created us to be. During this time of puberty, it is a preparation for a future vocation; the particular way God has called a person to fulfill His mission. The loving guidance provided within the family is especially important and influential in this maturation process. Thank God that He sent His only Son not only to teach us, but also to show us through His own life. He began life in a family where He witnessed and experienced the type of self-sacrificing love He Himself would show for mankind to the fullest measure in His redemptive mission. By looking to Jesus and relying on His grace, we can become the man or woman God created us to be.

How To Talk With Your Son

(The experience of this author is that the appropriate time for discussing human sexuality with your son is later than that required for one's daughter simply because she may well start her period as early as the fifth grade. Your son may be a couple years older before such a discussion is required. The approach taken below reflects this difference. You have the option to discuss the marital act with your son in a fuller context as set forth in subsequent pages.)

1. Male Biology: Physical Changes

Puberty is the time in a young man's life when his body starts to undergo physical changes. Every young man throughout the centuries has gone through puberty and you will also. These physical changes in the body usually begin in the early teenage years -- around the age you are now. So, it's time to talk about what these changes are and what they mean as you begin to grow into a young man.

These physical changes in your body happen because there is an increase in the level of hormones in your body. You will begin to notice the growth of hair on your face, in your armpits, and in your crotch area, referred to as "pubic hair." Your voice will also begin to deepen and, in the transition to a deeper voice, you may go through a period where your voice "cracks." "Cracking" is where the tonal quality of your voice fluctuates (even in the course of a single sentence) between high and low sounds. Eventually, your voice will stabilize at a deeper level, but in the process, it may seem awkward. Just recognize that a changing voice is part of the normal transition to manhood and will not last long.

As these changes happen, it is important to pay closer attention to your personal hygiene. For example, body odor becomes more noticeable and your skin and hair become oilier. This necessitates bathing or showering each day as well as the daily use of deodorant.

Puberty is also a time when your sexual organs, **genitals***, begin to grow. You will begin to notice an enlargement of your penis, scrotum, and testicles. As you can see in Diagram C, page 69 the most apparent male sex organ is the* **penis***, which is located in front of the* **scrotum***. The scrotum is a sac of loose skin containing two, small, ball-like objects called* **testicles***. The testicles produce the male hormone called testosterone. It is the increase of testosterone in the body, which causes the body to undergo various physical changes. Sperm are produced by the testicles,* **testes***, located in the scrotum. The sperm leave the testicles through a small tube called the vas deferens. The sperm are carried in a milky-like fluid called semen and passed through the urethra, which is the passageway inside the penis. While urine is also passed through the penis, the ability to urinate is blocked when sperm are released such that the two never occur at the same time.*

25

(If you should ever notice anything like ongoing pain lasting for several days or more, or anything like lumps in the testicle area, you should tell your father or mother. It might be something that needs treatment.)

You will become increasingly aware that your sexual organs are changing for some very practical reasons:

First, as a result of hormonal changes in your body, you may find your penis becoming enlarged or erect (stiff) for no apparent reason. This erection can cause awkwardness and sometimes discomfort. In such situations it is best to relax and not think about it until the sensation subsides. Physical or mental activity, such as playing at a sport, or even taking a walk, usually causes the erection to subside. Even using your imagination to picture yourself in a very risky situation, e.g., walking around on a steel girder on the 40th floor of a building under construction will do the same thing.

Second, you may begin to have "wet dreams." During the course of sleep at night you may experience a short burst of semen squirting from your penis. This short burst is called an ejaculation. It is caused by a buildup of fluid that needs releasing in a way similar to urine. It is sometimes referred to as a "wet dream" simply because the ejaculation leaves a wet spot on your pajamas or bedclothes. The discharge of semen may or may not be caused by a dream stimulating your sex organs. Nevertheless, this discharge of semen is beyond your control. It is a normal occurrence likely to happen at various times in the years to come.

2. Male and Female Sex Organs

To grasp the beauty of human sexuality, you also need to understand how the sex organs of the female body work. In looking at Diagram A, page 65 you can see the female sex organs, which unlike the male are located inside her body.

Inside each ovary are tiny eggs called ova. When a young girl begins puberty, about once a month one of these tiny eggs is released into her fallopian tube. As it begins to travel down the fallopian tube, the lining of the uterus begins to build itself up with blood and fluid to provide the proper environment for the egg should it become fertilized. If the egg is not fertilized, it and the blood and fluid that have built up the wall lining the uterus are discharged through her vagina at the end of her monthly cycle. This is also called her period or menstrual cycle. At this time she will wear some form of sanitary protection to catch the blood as it comes out.

When the egg is fertilized, it becomes a baby. The physical process of fertilizing an egg occurs when a husband inserts his penis into his wife's vagina and through ejaculation releases sperm. This is called sexual intercourse, an act of love that belongs to them alone. (The sacramental nature of sexual intercourse act is discussed over the next few pages.) This is the act that God has designed for a husband and wife to express the total commitment of love and dedication they expressed in their marriage vows. If the husband's sperm comes in contact with his wife's egg, the egg becomes fertilized and a baby is created. The baby will grow in her uterus for about nine months. After this period her cervix will open up and her uterus will start contracting and push the baby out of her body through her vagina.

3. God's Plan and Purpose

Human sexuality, both male and female, is good because God gave it to us. It is no accident that men and women become attracted to one another as they mature with age. It is part of God's plan that males and females are attracted to each other -- so much so that they will want to get married and start new families, thereby continuing God's plan of creation. Think what would happen if men and women were not attracted to one another -- they would not get married and human life as God planned it would cease.

The most intimate expression of our human sexuality occurs in sexual intercourse. Sexual intercourse is a gift from God reserved exclusively for husband and wife in marriage. It is called the "marriage act" and through it God shares with husband and wife the most awesome and most beautiful power to create a new human life by bringing a new baby into the world. God has specifically limited the sharing of this gift to a husband and wife to allow them to grow in mutual love of one another and to enable them to bring children into this world in the nurturing environment of a family.

To make it absolutely clear that sexual intercourse is reserved solely for husband and wife in marriage. God gave us the sixth and ninth commandments, and He demands that we obey them. The sixth commandment is: "You shall not commit adultery." That word "adultery" is related to the word, "adulterate," which means, "water down, weaken, or make cheap." The commandment means that a person must not lessen or cheapen the sexual gift he has saved for the expression of love between a husband and wife in marriage.

4. Adherence to God's Plan

It is important that you respect both your own sexuality and the sexuality of others. We are all required to control our thoughts, words, and actions so as to lead pure and chaste lives. But what does this means to you, as you become a young adult?

Dignity and Respect: *It means that you are required to uphold the dignity of human sexuality for both men and women as God intended. It means that in your thoughts, words, and conduct you must not cheapen or detract from what God has made beautiful. It means that you show others by your example to respect the sexuality of a woman and to protect her purity. It means those jokes, language, pictures, movies, or behaviors that detract from or* make fun of the beauty of God's gift of human sexuality are inappropriate. It means that you must be sensitive to the fact that a woman must accept her monthly cycle, or period, along with the discomfort and inconvenience it entails, and also be respectful of the fundamental role it plays in bringing new life into the world. It means that your attitude, speech, and behavior must enlighten others -- to encourage and help other young men and women to appreciate the dignity and purpose of the sexuality God has bestowed upon them and to respect it.

Vigilance: You must always be vigilant in this regard. One of the things our Blessed Mother said when she appeared at Fatima is that sins of impurity are what most often lead people to suffer the loss of their souls. As you advance through puberty, and throughout the course of your life, your sexual desires and urges may at times be very strong. God will give you all the help you need to lead a pure and chaste life. You need only to ask for His help in prayer and to avoid situations that might lead you or someone else to offend God. In addition, you should constantly ask our Blessed Mother for her help. Jesus hears and answers in a special way the requests of His Mother when she intercedes on our behalf in asking her Son for the graces we need to lead pure and chaste lives.

Control and Responsibility: You must control your conduct. It means that you treat a girl in the same manner that you would demand of any young man attracted to your sister. The media and many forces in society constantly tell young people to be as "sexy" as possible and to use their sexuality in any way they want. God says respect yourself and the dignity He has bestowed upon you in making you in His image and likeness. Others may tell you differently and lead lives contrary to how God Himself has told us to live. You must always remember that you, and only you -- not someone else, are responsible and accountable before God for your actions. You must always have the desire and the courage to protect and preserve your virginity as a gift for your future wife in marriage, and to protect and preserve a young woman's virginity as a gift for her future husband in marriage.

Prudence: You must always be prudent in the example you set for others. Make sure that your conduct never misleads others or allows others to disparage your reputation or the reputation of a young woman, or otherwise detract from the witness you provide to the message of Christ in living your life in a pure and chaste manner.

Compassion: Adherence to God's plan also requires that you are compassionate toward other people who may give in to their human weaknesses and misuse their sexuality causing them to fail to lead pure and chaste lives. Your help must show forgiveness, compassion, and respect.

5. Growth is Gradual

There is so much to growing up and so much to look forward to in the process. Thank God that He stretches it out for us by not asking us to grow up all at one time. It's important to enjoy where you are at each age and not try to rush it, because you will never be that age again. You know that growing up won't always be easy, but nothing very worthwhile in life is easy. It is a wonderful and challenging time -- and, of course, it goes on forever, because we never stop growing up!

This is a continuing process of maturing into the man or woman God created us to be. During this time of puberty, it is a preparation for a future vocation; the particular way God has called a person to fulfill His mission. The loving guidance provided within the family is especially important and influential in this maturation process. Thank God that He sent His only Son not only to teach us, but also to show us through His own life. He began life in a family where He witnessed and experienced the type of self-sacrificing love He Himself would show mankind to the fullest measure in His redemptive mission. By looking to Jesus and relying on His grace, we can become the man or woman God created us to be.

II. SPOUSAL LOVE REFLECTS THE LOVE OF CHRIST FOR EACH ONE OF US IN THE EUCHARIST

Note: Theme II and Theme III make reference to our union in Christ as the Mystical Body, the Church. A simple way of understanding the Mystical Body is from the cross. At the moment Christ's physical body died, His Mystical Body, the Church was born and awaited its baptism by the Holy Spirit on Pentecost.

"The Catholic Church, founded by Christ, began at the time of His death and Resurrection. Through His death and Resurrection, Jesus earned for us the privilege of belonging to God's family, the Church. To enter that family we need sanctifying grace, a sharing in the life of Christ, which we first receive when we are baptized.

By the power of Baptism, we become members of the Church, the Mystical Body of Christ. Thus, we become united to one another through our union with Christ, Who is the Head of the Body. Incorporated into Christ, we are freed from sin's dominion."

(*The Apostolate's Family Catechism*, Abridged One-Volume Edition, by Rev. Lawrence G. Lovasik. S.V.D., p. 286

Analogy to Christ's Love

Husband and wife love each other totally in a way that is like the love that Jesus has for us in the Eucharist. The following analogy may help to understand and appreciate in greater fullness the beauty of marital love:

Love in the Eucharist

Christ's love in the Eucharist is a total gift of self. Jesus unites totally with us as we unite totally with Him and offer our bodies as His home. We have united ourselves to Him in the Mass. All our joys and sufferings, our good times and our bad, our thoughts, prayers, work, play, and routines of each day are united in Him. (The priest gives a visible sign of this when He pours water into the cup during the preparation of gifts. The water is a sign that from our baptism, we are members of Christ's Mystical Body.) The love is a total sharing of our lives with His.

Jesus recognizes and loves our individuality and freedom. He sacrificed Himself for each one of us as individuals. He knows that our diversity is needed to keep His Church strong. Our love for Him grows because of this.

Jesus actually becomes absorbed into our bodies so that He becomes a part of us and allows us to become more a part of Him.

The love of Christ in the Eucharist is sacramental and life-giving. He gives us His life of grace and with this new life we gain strength to do His work in the world.

The Eucharist is our nourishment that unites us with every member of the Church; the people at Mass receiving with us and the entire Mystical Body. We unite with each other to build up the Body of Christ.

After receiving Jesus, He then sends us on our way into the world to do His work -- always reminding us that His love for us will never end.

Love in Marriage

Love between husband and wife is a total gift of self. Husband unites totally with his wife and she unites totally with him as she receives him into her body. Husband and wife unite all that they are before God. They share all their joys and sufferings, good times and bad, thoughts, prayers, work, play, and routines of each day. Their love is a total sharing of their lives.

Husband and wife respect each others individuality and freedom. This often means sacrificing one's own wishes for a greater good. Their diversity is what keeps the family strong and their love grows because of this.

Husband becomes absorbed into his wife's body. The two become one and are parts of each other.

The love of husband and wife is sacramental and life-giving. They receive the life of grace which gives them strength to do God's work in the family and in the world. And, with the union of sperm and egg, they literally cooperate with God to give NEW LIFE.

Husband and wife, nourished by their love, unite with each other to build up the Body of Christ by bringing new members into the Body. Then, all contribute to building up the Body of Christ in the world.

Husband and wife send their children into the world, nourished by their love, to do God's work -- always reminding them that their love for them will never end.

A Husband's Love

"Husbands, love your wives even as
Christ loved the Church and handed
Himself over for her..." (Eph.5:25)

"Husbands love your wives," love them because of that special and unique bond whereby in marriage a man and a woman become "one flesh." (Gn. 2:24, Eph. 5:31) (John Paul II, On the Dignity and Vocation of Women)

Christ so loves the Church that He gave Himself up for her by dying on a cross. He so loves the Church that He continues to give Himself in absolute unity with her. The Church is Christ's Mystical Body in which He draws all baptized people into complete union with Himself. He continues to give Himself totally to each member of the Body in the Eucharist. Through these sacraments, He first incorporates us into His Body and then turns around and submits to become part of our bodies. His abundant graces enable our growth in holiness.

Just as Christ gave Himself up for the Church, a husband is called to give himself up for his wife and sacrifice for her. He must give himself completely to his wife and to no other woman. His love, like Christ's love for the Church, is to be sacrificial and self-giving. His love for his wife should bring him closer to Christ and should be an avenue of graces enabling their growth in holiness.

A Wife's Love

"Be subordinate to one another out of reverence for Christ. Wives
should be subordinate to their husbands as to the Lord. For the
husband is head of his wife just as Christ is head of the church, he
himself the savior of the body." (Eph. 5: 21-23)

"Be subject to one another out of reverence for Christ." The gift of self necessarily demands the sacrifice of one's own desires in love and obedience to those of Christ. Christ, their constant companion and guide, is the bonding force of their union. As Christ is head of the Church, the husband is head of his wife and family.

Complementary to her husband, who is the head, the wife is the heart of their union. As Christ died for the Church and submitted to the will of His Father, so a husband sacrifices himself for his wife, and she, in turn, through the same gift of self, sacrifices herself for him.

"The wife can and should find in her relationship with Christ – Who is the one Lord for both spouses – the motivation of the relationship with her husband which flows from the very essence of marriage and the family… The husband and the wife are in fact 'subject to one another', and are mutually subordinated to one another. The source of this mutual subjection is to be found in Christian pietas, (reverence for Christ), and its expression is love." (Pope John Paul II, August 11, 1982 audience)

Christ as the very center and glue of their marriage is constantly present to both husband and wife who must always look to one another for wisdom and guidance. In this way they will be united in their goals and decisions. The head and the heart must necessarily act as one or "one" will not survive. As our model, in His plan for salvation, God worked through Joseph as head of the holy family and through Mary, its heart. In mutual submission to one another their love for God came first, and so through this holy family, Christ came into our world. Submission here does not mean subjugation, but refers to a much greater love that means sacrificing one's own pride and comfort for a greater good that conforms to the plan of God. In imitation of the holy family, every family's mission is to bring Christ into the world. Submission is demanding, but it is equally demanding of both spouses. "Be subordinate to one another out of reverence for Christ." (Eph. 5:21)

This is a difficult passage for many. It implies humility. Just as husbands must practice humility through sacrifice and self-giving, so also must wives. Humility is **truth**. It is the truth as God sees it. It is recognizing strengths and weaknesses as gifts from God. It is recognizing the beauty of masculinity and femininity as equal and complementary gifts. It is trusting in God's wisdom. It is relying on Him as children. It is using His gifts to honor Him and build His kingdom through the vocation to which He calls each person. In matrimony, wives are called to be the **heart** of the union, just as husbands are called to be the **head**. The head and the heart are the most visible and crucial signs of life for the body. Neither is superior but complementary because "Love excludes every kind of subjection … Love makes the husband simultaneously subject to the wife, and thereby subject to the Lord himself, just as the wife to the husband." (*August 11, 1982 Audience*). The two, united with God, function intimately together.

Fulton Sheen compares God to the architect who designs a building. As the designer, he knows every detail about his building. The truth about ourselves is that God, as our Creator, knows us to the very detail. He knows every strength and weakness better than we know them ourselves. A husband and wife must love each other by accepting each other's strengths and weaknesses and using them as a means to grow closer to God and bring others to Him, too. The love of husband and wife must, therefore, be humble in order to build on each other's strengths and even to recognize that every weakness offers an opportunity for growth in holiness.

Their Different Roles

We saw that, like the Trinity, all have distinctive roles within the family. The husband and father is head of the family and its "support system" in all its implications. As the heart of the family, the wife and mother's is a nurturing role, and a wondrous role it is. Holy mothers nurture their sons and encourage them to become holy priests and brothers, holy fathers, and holy men who work in the world and influence others. Holy mothers nurture their daughters and encourage them to become consecrated women, holy mothers, and holy women who work in the world and influence others. Wives turn to their husbands for support and reinforcement both for themselves and for their children. Fathers are the heads of families. But mothers are first to nurture those future fathers from the moment of conception. If we want good and holy men, we must have good and holy mothers! We need holy fathers who are spiritual heads of their families.

Even Christ, Lord and High Priest, looked to His mother for love and guidance. It was she who nurtured Him, taught Him the Scriptures and His prayers, brought Him home from the temple when He was twelve, and directed His first miracle at age thirty to begin His redemptive mission. She placed all confidence in God as did her husband, Joseph. She is the model of femininity for all women. God glorified her role as wife and mother and made her Queen of Heaven, Mother of us all. In fact, she is the model for all Christians. All the great saints who have ever lived, both male and female, have looked to her for loving guidance and intercedence. There is no one closer to the Trinity than Mary; no one more in love with the Trinity than Mary; no one who knows the Trinity more intimately than Mary. She is daughter to the Father, mother to the Son, and spouse to the Holy Spirit. She shared intimately in the sufferings of our Savior and, therefore, shared in our redemption. God chose her Himself and blessed her from among all women of all time. From the cross, He gave her to us as our mother. It only makes sense that we should turn to her. Children do seem to always run to their mothers first!

The Marriage Gift

(The following provides you with the words to use in order to present your child with a beautifully simple but accurate explanation of marital love, intercourse. You may decide to do this immediately following the discussion about the changes in the body, OR you may decide your child is not quite ready and save this for a more suitable time. You know your child best. When the time is right, relax and enjoy this special moment. Your child may react in any number of ways. Keep in mind that no reaction is right or wrong. In fact, you may want to share your own reaction when you were first told. Most importantly, simply reassure your child of the beauty of God's gift. He/she may not understand but will hear you and remember your time together.)

You know that mom and dad love you very much -- more than anyone else on earth! There is nobody that comes close to loving you the way that we do. Yet, Jesus loves you infinitely more times than this -- so much so that our minds can never comprehend it.

*Jesus loves us **all** so much that He never wants to be separated from us. This is why He gives us the gift of baptism making each one of us a part of His Mystical Body, the Church. As members of His Body, we actually live inside of Him. Now, here's the kicker -- He loves us SO much that **He wishes to live inside of us, too**. This is His gift of **Holy Eucharist**. Now, think: We love each other very much, and we can hold each other closely. We can squeeze each other tightly, and more tightly, and as tightly as we can in a huge bear hug. But, that is as close as we can get. Jesus, on the other hand, can do the impossible! Because He is God, He can make Himself our food and come, **body and soul**, into our bodies. No two human beings can be THIS close! He even wishes to become a **part of us** because, as food He is absorbed into our bodies. He really does become a part of us, and we become more a part of Him because of what we share. This is a love we cannot imagine: While He lives inside of us, we continue to live inside of Him. It is a bond so tight that it is far beyond our understanding! It is love beyond our understanding.*

*Now, imagine this: God has given a gift of love to husband and wife that is a little like this love that He shows us in Communion. Of course, it is **not just** like it, or even close, but it is the closest thing we have on earth that physically resembles it. And, **He has given this awesome gift to husband and wife in the Sacrament of Matrimony! What a sacred and precious gift it is!!!***

*This special gift of love between husband and wife is called **spousal love** or **marital love**. The physical aspect of marital love is called **intercourse**. The word, intercourse, actually means a communication between people. When referring to the expression of physical love, it means **the most intimate kind** of communication between two people, husband and wife. Scripture actually refers to it as knowledge. Mary said, "I do not know man." ("Making love" and "having sex" are two very common expressions for intercourse. However, one or perhaps both of these expressions seem to separate the physical part of love from all the other parts. This was never God's intention.)*

Intercourse

(See Diagram C, page 69, to follow the sperm path with your son/daughter.)

*This is a special time of closeness for husband and wife. They will now give themselves to each other in body and spirit in the presence of God. They hold each other close and show their affection for one another. While they are loving one another in this way, something begins to happen inside the body of the husband. Notice where the sperm are now. They will leave this area (the testicle) and begin to swim through the long tube (the vas deferens). As the sperm are swimming along this path, the penis begins to harden and elongate and receive the first sperm. Husband and wife continue to express their love through signs of affection. Both of their bodies are preparing to be together. The husband's penis now becomes very hard and stiff and is filled with many, many sperm. (Now, refer to Diagram A, page 65, of the female body.) The wife's vagina has also prepared itself by becoming warm and moist. When the time is right for both of them, the wife receives her husband into her body; his penis, hard and stiff, slips right into the vagina of his wife. "And, the two become one body." They are united in such a way that no other two people can appreciate, because their union is unique! They give to each other before God in body and spirit. To their union, they bring all their joys and sorrows, their struggles, their good times and bad times, etc. **All that they are** as individuals become one as they are now one.*

Now, how does a baby happen? At some point, the sperm will release from the penis and swim into the vagina and up the fallopian tubes. If this is a time when an egg is making its way down the path, it is possible for one of the sperm to enter it. If this happens, the egg will change its character to "signal" that fertilization has taken place. It is now impossible for another sperm to enter the egg. This union of sperm and egg is a tiny, tiny baby. The baby now finds that nice warm spot that mom has prepared and nestles in, by attaching to the wall of the uterus. Here, the baby will begin to grow and develop until ready for birth in about nine months.

There are many good resources for looking at pictures of a developing baby (I suggest "Watch Me Grow" in the Bibliography). You can also explain how the body readies itself for the birth and how the baby is born through the vagina, which has now become the birth canal. (If you are asked about pain, be honest. Everything worthwhile in life involves some pain, and this is certainly no exception.) But, the "pay-off" here is extraordinary! What a tremendous gift to be able to work with God to bring another one of His children into the world. And, this child (your child), He has entrusted to you!!!

III. SPOUSAL LOVE IS SACRAMENTAL LOVE

Marriage is a Sacrament

What is a sacrament? The traditional definition from *The Baltimore Catechism*: "A sacrament is an **outward sign**, instituted by Christ to give grace." A good and holy priest described it to me another way, i.e., "as a human event within the life of the Church in which Jesus is present saving the world." St. Paul tells us that

> *"For no one hates his own flesh, but rather nourishes and cherishes it; even as Christ does the Church, because we are members of his body. For this reason, a man must leave (his) father and (his) mother and be joined to his wife, and the two shall become one flesh."* (Eph. 5: 29-32)

Scripture tells us that spousal love is a **sign** of Christ's love for the Church. The love between husband and wife is a **sensible sign** (i.e. visible to our senses) of the most intimate love that Christ has for us; a **sign** of **total self-giving**. The two become one in marriage. The two (Christ and His people) become one in the Church, the Mystical Body of Christ. The two (Christ and communicant) become one in the Eucharist.

Marriage was first given as a gift from God to Adam and Eve at the very start of creation. Jesus reaffirmed that gift to us when He came as man and elevated marriage to a most sacred state.

During the marriage feast at Cana, Jesus performed the first sign of Himself, *revealing Who He is in all His glory.* This was the beginning of His redemptive work and also the beginning of Mary's co-redemptive role. He is the **New Adam** and she is the **New Eve**. It is the beginning of the **New Creation**! Although the bride and groom must have been close friends of Jesus and Mary, the couple remains anonymous. We don't know their names, and that gives universality to what happened there! In essence, every married couple is the wedding couple at Cana. In essence, every married couple is the beginning of a new creation!

Through the grace of the sacrament, married couples receive all the help they need. This couple invited Jesus to be a part of their marriage, but didn't even realize what miracle had taken place. They didn't realize that when Jesus is invited, miracles are bound to happen.

In Matthew 19: 1-9, Mark 10: 1-12, and Luke 16: 18, Jesus firmly states that marriage is indissoluble. He explains that Moses, in the Old Covenant allowed divorce because the heart of man was hardened. But, this is the New Covenant. *"Now I say to you: whoever divorces his wife ... and marries another commits adultery."* Jesus was reaffirming marriage as committed love, a love that is forever, a sign of His own love. That is, He elevated marriage to a sacrament giving the couple all the necessary graces to fulfill their vocation.

Grace, being a share in the very life of God Himself, is without question bestowed abundantly on the couple as a constant source of comfort, support, and strength for their mission in the world. Marriage takes three. Husband and wife take their vows before God and His Church. He is the third Person and the cement of the marriage.

Husband and wife become cooperators with God in the very act of bringing new life into the world. Into this new life, God breathes an immortal soul, made in His image and likeness. It is an awesome share in the very essence of God's life and love. God has then entrusted to husband and wife the awesome responsibility of nurturing their child, His child, to a faith-filled maturity. God does not expect married couples to accomplish all this on their own. Just as He was present at their vows and at the conception of their children, He remains present within the marriage as *the* Source of life and love for the continued growth of the family. This is an abundant gift of grace!

When husband and wife love each other deeply and want desperately to share that love with children, but are unable to bear children of their own, they seek God's help to accept their cross. They look to the Source of life for the children they cannot bear, and God looks on them with His *grace* and compassion. He knows that their love for each other is not selfish, but is sacrificial and self-giving. He will help them know how to share that love with others. Whether they decide to adopt children, or choose to serve other members of God's family, the same sacramental graces are always abundant, just for the asking. As He was present long ago with the couple in Cana, in all His glory, He remains present with couples today. He blessed the marriage in Cana by *sharing a part of Himself* with them and He has extended that gift to all in the sacrament of matrimony!

There are seven sacraments. The final reason for that

> "...is hidden in the mind of God. But humanly speaking we can say there are seven sacraments because they correspond in things of the spirit to the needs we have in the order of nature. We must be born in the life of grace by baptism, strengthened in this life by confirmation, nourished to sustain the supernatural life by the Eucharist, healed by the sacrament of penance, guided in the supernatural society of the Church by priests who receive holy orders, the Church is perpetuated by the sacrament of matrimony, and we are prepared for eternity by the sacrament of anointing." (*The Question and Answer Catholic Catechism*, John A. Hardon, S.J.)

The Church is *the* Great Sacrament; it is Christ present in the world. Before His arrest, Jesus prayed for His disciples and for His Church:

> *"Holy Father, keep them in your name that you have given me so that they may be one, even as we are ... As you sent me into the world, so I send them into the world; And I consecrate myself for them, that they also may be consecrated in truth."* (John 17:11, 18-19)

He prayed that His Church be an image of the Trinity and He gave Himself up for that purpose.

In the Scriptures, He tells us that the union of husband and wife is an image of both the Church and the Trinity. In *awe*, every man and woman (for all are graced in some way) can thank God for His most precious gift of the Sacrament of Matrimony.

THOUGHTS TO CONSIDER

(Use these thoughts as you wish to reinforce ideas with an older child. They follow in the order of the three themes, but a reading of the entire text is necessary for good reflection. It may also be helpful to have a Bible, a Lives of the Saints, and the *Catechism of the Catholic Church* at your side for reference. Numbers referring to selections in the Catechism are indicated and may be helpful for reflection and understanding.)

Reflections: I. Spousal love reflects the love of the Trinity

Image and Likeness

1.   Notice the word "our" before image and before likeness. Consider for a moment: What would happen to the existence of God and the world if any One Person of the Three ceased to exist? Consider the **bond** and the **commitment** of that kind of love, a love so intense that it makes three Persons One God, a mystery beyond our human comprehension. Consider it in Their Own unity and in Their unity with man, especially the extraordinary bond created with us through each of the sacraments. God's love cannot be contained. It eternally overflows by its very strength and nature. In Baptism, He makes His home within the human soul. In the Eucharist, He goes even farther and makes His home within the human body. First, consider Their roles in completion of the Godhead. Next, consider Their roles in completion of life and love in the world. (253-260, 2331-2334, 1118)

If we, as individuals and as family, are made in the image and likeness of God, then the way we love should image the way God loves. When we show love to others, they should see His goodness. What does it say about the casual use of the word, "love," in our society? (355-357, 372-373, 1604)

What does it say about the casual use of sex in our society? Take the word, "sex," and society's use of it. When the word is spoken, is its immediate connotation that of committed love? -- or spousal love? (1605, 2360-2363)

In society, does the word "sex" readily connote the fullness and beauty of masculinity and femininity? What does it mean to be truly a man? -- truly a woman? Who can we look to as models of true masculinity and femininity? (2331-2336)

Reverence for the sacredness of sexuality begins at an early age within the family. As we mature, we are influenced by others as well as family. We also begin to make our own decisions, using the freedom that God gave us. In order to use that freedom wisely and for the good of others, we need to keep our conscience informed at every age. How can we acquire and keep a well-formed conscience? (1783-1789, 2039)

The freedom that God gave us is a freedom to choose -- to choose love for Him or self-centered love. In which of these would we find true freedom? (1731-1738, 1742, 2339, 2548-2550)

2. What is a mystery? Why is love such a great mystery? Do you think we are mysteries even to ourselves? To others? How does this affect our relationships with family and friends, both male and female? (36-38) (826, 1827) (221, 227, 733-736) (1822-1827)

3. God created the world and everything in it with a *plan* in mind. The basic plan was to make the world an extension of Himself. So, we should see His greatness and goodness in every living creature. In His image, He set mankind over all the rest and entrusted him with the care of His creation. The creation of man was Gods' masterpiece. Would you say that mankind fills that position? (41, 299, 358, 2401-2449)

Isn't it interesting that the lower animals "mate" in much the same way as humans? It does make sense because they, too, are expressions of God. Even the animals were not made to be alone. They were made for each other, to perpetuate their species. And they were made for us, to lighten our burden. But, the key word here is "mate." Animals mate. Human beings *love*. God raised us to a higher level by giving us an immortal soul, like His own. Then, in baptism, He fills it with His grace and gives us a share in His divine life. What food for thought does this provide with respect to the meaning of human sexuality? (460, 505, 1265, 1617)

4. God has given us the gift of love to enjoy for a lifetime and longer. "Faith, hope, and charity, and the greatest of these is charity." Faith and hope belong to this world. But, charity lives on into the next. We will *never* stop loving. Will we ever stop growing in love? What does this do to your idea of heaven? of the magnificence of God? (1023-1029)

Family Love Resembles God's Love

5. Love is *knowing* someone and *wanting* to know that someone better. Love is *choosing* to do what you *think* is good for another person. Love is *giving* of yourself without counting the cost, large or small. Love is *thinking* of the other person before yourself. What do you observe about people who are "in love?" Consider the routines of daily life, as well as special times and difficult situations. Often, true love shines forth best in the trials of life. Why do you think this is so? (1642-1643, 1648, 1661-1662) Does it help you to better understand Christ's gift of Himself on the cross? Does it help to understand that the crosses He sends us are gifts? (1769)

Respect for Our Bodies

6. Have you ever thought about the real meaning of *love* at its *source*, God Himself? God is *all-loving.* There is no amount of love anywhere in heaven or on earth that comes remotely close to the depths of His love for us. Now think: Who is God? He is a Spirit having intellect and will. He has no human body nor human feelings or emotions. Now think about your idea of love. Do a lot of feelings and emotions readily come to mind? These are human *expressions* of love and very precious gifts from God that He has given to us to enjoy! But, *are they true love*? If our love reflects God's love, then it must come from the soul, the intellect and will (like His); knowledge and choice. Love, then, is an *action of the soul*. Our feelings and emotions are expressions of that love! The body expresses love in a language all its own and through this expression of love brings God, Who is Love itself into our world. The body is the **visual expression** of the soul. What does that say about the holiness of the body? (362-367, 1704-1709, 1762, 1766-1770)

(A word of caution: If not embedded in true love, our emotions can be deceiving. We must guard against something that just "feels good." Let the well-formed conscience in your soul be your guide.) (1768)

Growth is Gradual

7.   Growing up is a process that takes a lifetime. It is a process of body, mind, and soul. As did Jesus, we grow in wisdom, age, and grace before God and man. Growth is a process of our entire being, each of us unique in the eyes of God. He blessed each of us with special qualities for which He designed our unique purpose for living. So, of course, growth in the realization, development, and use of these talents is vitally important and obligatory. Look at the parable of the talents in Matthew 25: 14-30. How does it relate to the following passage, 25: 31-46, on the last judgment?

At every age, whether young or old, it is necessary to serve others in every way available to us. The spiritual and corporal works of mercy provide us with a wonderful guide to the various ways possible. A careful look will indicate that it is possible to serve well without doing extraordinary things. (2447) Where do your particular talents fit in? (1913-1914, 1944-1946, 1948, 1971-1974)

Reflections: II. Spousal love reflects the love of Christ for each one of us in the Eucharist

A Husband's and Wife's Love

1. Christ gave Himself up for us on the cross. He continues to unite Himself with us in the Eucharist. He gives us Himself as the Church, His Mystical Body. We accomplish all things through Him (the cross), with Him (the Eucharist), and in Him (the Mystical Body). He is our strength (cross), our nourishment (Eucharist), our unity, and our support (Mystical Body). *The Mass is Christ's greatest act of love.* Reflect on the above ideas within the context of the Mass. Why should the Mass be *the center of our lives* as individuals, as family, and as community? (864, 1088, 1324, 1373-1374)

Their Different Roles

2. Humility is Truth; the truth about ourselves as God sees us. In Fr. Hardon's *Catholic Dictionary*, humility "is the virtue that restrains the unruly desire for personal greatness and leads people to an orderly love of themselves based on a true appreciation of their position with respect to God and their neighbors. *Religious humility recognizes one's total dependence on God; moral humility recognizes one's creaturely equality with others*. Yet humility is not only opposed to pride; it is also opposed to immoderate self-abjection, which would fail to recognize God's gifts and use them according to his will." Humility, then, recognizes both strengths and weaknesses. To deny either would only work against God and His plan because we build on both to attain holiness and to fulfill our mission. Does this change your idea about humility? How does it encourage you to fulfill the purpose for which you were created? (1697, 2587, 2606)

    Do you think it is important to ask God daily for the grace to know your vocation in life and for the grace to fulfill that vocation according to His holy will? (791, 798, 836)

3. There is much talk about the role of women in the Church. Jesus shows us in Scripture that He considers women to have a very special role in building up His Church. It was a woman to whom He first entrusted the *good news of the Resurrection, the single most important event in our history!* It was a woman to whom He first entrusted the *Good News of salvation*, and that same woman sits next to His throne as Queen. (If you recall, this was a position sought by some of the apostles. But, only Mary could drink from the same cup as Christ!) Through Mary, we received Jesus. And, through Mary, we receive the graces that He won for us. (618, 964, 967-969)

    Jesus entrusts His Word first to women, who are the first carriers of this Good News to others. Mary is the first role model for all women. Can you think of others in Scriptures, or perhaps in the lives of the saints, or even in the lives of great women who have made a real difference in the world? How did these women fulfill a role of motherhood in the world?

    Because of the Ascension, Jesus resides in heaven in body and soul, as God and as man. Because of the Assumption, Mary, who is fully human, resides in heaven in both body and soul. From all of mankind, **Mary** is the only one given this privilege by God. The Trinity chose Mary as the beginning of the New Creation. What does this say about the Trinity's love and respect for womanhood and motherhood? What does it say about the Trinity's love and respect for the human body? (966, 972-975)

4. Jesus willed to be born from an earthly Mother. He willed that this same Mother be the first to guide His footsteps in growing up. It was His Mother who stepped in when He was 12 and let Him know that His time had not yet come. (Perhaps, like most children that age, Jesus was anxious to grow up!) And then at 30, when He resisted, it was His Mother who directed the waiter to "do whatever He tells you." It was His Mother who shared His redemptive mission in suffering and in glory!

    Jesus, Lord and High Priest, looked to His Mother for guidance and consolation. He then wanted His first priests to have the same guidance and consolation (and intercedence). That is why Mary remained in their midst until the Holy Spirit came, and then, remained as Mother of the Church. Jesus intends this for all of His priests -- first from Mary, and also from their own holy mothers. Consider society's view of motherhood and its idea of success in the world. ("Behold Your Mother," the Holy Thursday Letter of John Paul II may be of interest here.) (489, 507, 721-726, 965, 973-975, 2204)

5. "Husbands should love their wives just as Christ loved the Church and sacrificed for her to make her holy." There is no better example than Mary's husband, Joseph. Joseph's love for Mary was self-surrendering from the very beginning. When found with Child, his concern was for her and his answer was from God. Joseph lived for love of God and his family. He was the head of the family responsible for the redemption of the world. How could he fulfill such an awesome responsibility? God always told him how, and no matter how incredible the answers were, Joseph trusted His Word. His wife and his Son relied on that strength of faith, trust, and love. (1639)

Can our world even begin to comprehend Joseph's position? It was Joseph's role to form Jesus as a man. He taught Him to be a carpenter and taught Him the value of work. From Joseph's example, Jesus learned the virtues needed to be a holy man among men and at home. Each day, Jesus witnessed His father's undying love for His mother. What part did he play in the mission of his family? He was the support pole. He was their support spiritually, emotionally, mentally, and physically. The work of Redemption began in a family and God asked Joseph to be its head, guaranteed of the necessary graces. (1642) (1602, 1603)

Can our world even comprehend Joseph's position? He was betrothed to the most beautiful woman that ever lived, the most loved of all women on earth and in heaven. Joseph loved Mary intensely. Because he was so intensely in love with her and with God, her gift of virginity became his gift, joyfully and generously given. It was truly a gift "for the sake of the kingdom of heaven." (1618 - 1620)

The Marriage Gift and Analogy to Christ's Love

6. Communion is "the act of sharing, or holding in common... (It is) an interchange or sharing of thoughts or emotions; **intimate** communication." (*Webster's Encyclopedic Dictionary*, the 1989 edition) Go back to the analogies of the "communion" between husband and wife to the "communion" between Christ and His people in the Mystical Body and in the Eucharist. (See pages 33 and 37). How are all of these intimate and sacred communications? Remember that Scripture refers to the marital act as knowledge of one another. (372, 1644)

Look particularly at the analogy of love in marriage to love in the Eucharist. Look at each step and think about the Church's teaching on birth control and God's design for family life and love, abortion and respect for life at all stages, pre-marital sex and the sacramental beauty of self-sacrificing marital love, cohabitation and committed, self-surrendering love, and the Church's teaching regarding homosexuality and the gift of marriage and family given to Adam and Eve "in Our image after Our likeness." The Church is the only source of such beauty, wisdom, knowledge, and truth! (Birth control, 2368-2378); (Abortion, 2270-2275, 1703, 357); (Premarital sex, 2353); (Homosexuality, 2357-2359); (Cohabitation, 2331, 2390-2391).

7.   Would you believe that in the days of the early Church, there were those who believed that sex was as necessary to the body as food and drink? Sound familiar to any present-day thinking? Reflect on the words of St. Paul in I Corinthians 6: 15-20.

Jesus "bought and paid for" us -- and a high price it was! We are His most precious possessions. Because we are His and He is in us, would He ever want us to USE our body or the body of another person for self-pleasure or self-gratification? As God's precious possessions, He intends that no one of us ever be used selfishly by anyone, including ourselves. For example, this is why masturbation and pornography are sinful. Selfish gratification is not an expression of love. Rather, it degrades the body as an object to be used for mere pleasure and entertainment. God made our passions and emotions good so that we would use them for good. God shows us His love and respect and asks that we show the same love and respect for ourselves and for others. He has created us for a noble purpose! (see page 47/48 #6.) (2351-2356, 2520-2527)

Dating

8.   Perhaps this is a good time for some talk with one another about dating. Socialization with the opposite sex is about making friends and having fun. Friends are people that we care about and respect. Having fun is important, but like all things it can get out of control if WE lose control. As with anything in life, helpful guidelines help ensure that it's fun and that it remains pleasing to God.

Dating is the process we use to find a future spouse. How unfortunate it would be to limit our choices by consciously choosing to narrow the field too early in the dating process. By approaching it one step at a time the years of adolescence are less pressured and more fun. Each step, from becoming acquainted within groups...to group activities...to group dating...to double dating...to single dating...to courtship and engagement, must be given proper time and attention. Here, too, growth remains gradual. We try at any age to treat our children in a way appropriate to their chronological and developmental years. No matter how old they are, we tend to watch from a guarded distance. We encourage growth, with guidance, a helping hand, and an open ear. Because the maturation process during adolescence is incomplete and still ongoing, this watchful eye remains crucial. Remember that growth is gradual, and as much as the process seems at times to want to accelerate, it's very prudent sometimes to ease up on the pedal. Too often it is the community and the larger society that encourage young people to relinquish so many childlike ways at so early an age. For example, in middle school when so many biological changes are taking place and awkwardness is so pronounced, why add to it by encouraging premature dating or pairing off through mixed parties and dances? We have very little control over the physical aspect of growth, but we do have some control over the social aspects. That control demands that we make choices, and when growing up, those choices are best made with the loving guidance of parents who can draw on their experience and the wisdom that comes with it. Parents need to set rules and guidelines to help ensure a fun and healthy social life. You can best decide what is appropriate for your family situation.

a.   Have you made any decisions regarding group, double, or single dating? (Remember, your teen may be using different words than you to describe the same thing.)

> Dating might begin in high school when the period of rapid physical growth has finally slowed down and your child has become somewhat accustomed to a new shape and to the care that goes along with a more adult looking body. The years of high school offer many chances for meeting new friends, especially through organized activities sponsored by school and community sports teams, mixers sponsored by schools and youth groups, and various other academic and charitable activities sponsored by schools, parishes, and communities. Rightfully so, *dating* might begin during the last two years of high school at a time when many *begin* to think into the future. By this time, most are getting or have already acquired driver's licenses, naturally accompanied by more freedom and more responsibility. During this time, group dating and double dating are certainly preferred as the logical step before single dating, courtship, and engagement. By dating with a group of friends,

there is more opportunity to expand interests, hobbies, and talents through conversation and activities. Steady dating necessarily means shutting out these possibilities and accepting only one input -- and, perhaps, only one output. It means expending a large amount of energy in a single direction towards one person. When energy levels are so high, what a wonderful time to develop the virtue of generosity at home, at school, in the parish, in the community, and among friends. Again, one step should build on and help prepare for the next. A solid and secure footing is really needed here to help prepare for the world they will meet after graduation.

b. How do you feel about girls calling boys on the telephone?

The male role is to **protect and to provide**. As husband and father, he will be the "head of his wife" (Ephesians 5: 21-33) and family. It doesn't just magically happen, but begins with the little things -- like having to make a phone call. Overcoming some sweaty palms or a nervous stomach can be a big first step. There are exceptions to this, of course, such as the prom at an all-girls' high school or Sadie Hawkins dances, but normally, the boy should initiate the phone call. By taking the initiative to call, he shows a willingness to assume some small amount of responsibility. By doing so he is more likely to accept a larger amount of responsibility and "protect" and "provide" for her when in her company. When a girl calls a boy she certainly feeds his ego, but is that the part of his masculinity she wants to feed? She also relieves him of initiative and responsibility. She has made it easy for him to be less of a man. Is that really what she wants to do? On the other hand, if he is the type of person she is looking for, he may even find her calls annoying.

c. What type of boy does she want to date?

Have you ever questioned why God created Adam first and alone? God wanted Adam to know and love Him first and to rely first and always on His guidance. This would be Adam's strength. He would then be the kind of man God wanted for Eve. When God is first everything else falls into place. Unfortunately, that isn't what happened. Adam did not turn to God for strength. His eyes were on Eve, but he failed to be the man he was called to be. He let her be tempted while he watched and did nothing. Then, he allowed himself to be tempted. Eve also failed to turn to God or to her husband. The consequences for both and for their future were grave.

Our culture so readily accepts that women can do anything men can do. While this is true to a great extent, this acceptance has led to a confusion of roles. We have forgotten the quite obvious, that God created man and woman equal but different and complementary. Men have lost sight of what it means to be a man. We need to help our young men regain their sight. We need to help our young women as well. Every woman wants a strong man; a man who respects her, who protects and cares for her. She wants someone who will help her to become a better person.

A note for both: How many times have you heard the proverbial question, "How far is too far?" The answer to that question is quite simple: If you are asking it, you may have already gone too far. You may have already turned onto the wrong road. Perhaps you are thinking, "How far can I push her/him to the edge of the cliff without actually throwing her/him off?" What you should be asking yourself is, "How can I best show respect for her/him as a person, as a child of God?" "**No**" can be a very loving word, and it can be said in many loving ways. Your dates, relationships and friendships should make you better persons and bring each of you closer to God.

d. Is it important for the boy to initiate the date, except in special circumstances?
   For the same reasons he should initiate the call, he should initiate the date. He is much more apt to approach that date with an attitude of respect and responsibility.

e. Is it important that the boy always pick the girl up at her house?
   This is simple courtesy. It also gives an opportunity to meet the girl's parents and know their expectations. It gives parents the opportunity to meet their daughter's dates. In fact, it is also important for a son to bring his date home to meet his parents. Relationships are always better when there is familiarity and open communication. How nice when a parent can say to a son or daughter, "How's 'so-and-so' doing?" with a familiarity of that person's interests and activities.

f. Is it important to first clear the date with mom or dad?
   Again, this is simple courtesy and shows consideration for others. There may also be an unknown conflict with the family schedule or calendar. There may be a conflict with Mom and Dad's plans. Perhaps you may be needed at home in some capacity. It may be hard to believe, but even parents must consider these things and others before making plans.

g. Is it important to have plans before leaving on a date?

> Of course, a night without plans can take many a wrong turn. Making plans is part of taking responsibility for the care of your date. For instance, something simple but perhaps important to the girl may be the need to know what she should wear. There is also a sense of security in knowing what is ahead. Most importantly, having no plans means having nowhere to go. A date with no plans should mean no date.

h. Are there any restrictions regarding places to go? Are there any restrictions regarding movies or concerts?

> In any community there are the obvious places to avoid. Any place referred to as a "hangout" would fall into this category. Even the name gives away its very lack of purpose and activity. Any secluded place, even the popular bike path, invites trouble simply due to the isolated nature of the place. Much of this is common sense. Remember safety rules. Never enter an apartment or a home with a boy where there is no one else present. Again, its isolated nature invites problems. In addition to isolated places and hangouts, avoid any place where under-aged drinking and/or drugs may be a problem. If there's trouble, the police won't ask questions. They take everyone. Even absent police, there's a situation asking for problems.

> Regarding movies: The Catholic News Service provides its own rating system for current and somewhat older movies. Go to www.catholicnews.com and click "Movie Reviews."

> Concerts should also be approached with much discretion due to the character of some musical groups and their lyrics and to the character of the crowds they attract.

i. Are parents home when your child is at someone's house?

> Yes, this is a necessary safeguard for all considered. However, parents also need to be vigilant whether it be a party or just a visit. Being present in and of itself is simply not enough, especially in today's world. Friends of the opposite sex should visit with one another only in the most common and visible areas of the house where there are others around. This presents a wonderful opportunity for parents and other family members to become better acquainted with their teen's/young adult's friends. Take full advantage of it!

j.   Should children always carry a cell phone and make sure it is charged?
     Should children call home if plans change?

> Again, this is simple courtesy. Parents can best establish this habit by setting the example and doing the same. Parents should call home and let children know if their plans change. It may prevent a lot of needless worry. Courtesy is courtesy no matter what the age.

k. What amount of money should a girl carry, just in case?

> A girl should always carry enough money for the price of a cab ride home. There should always be a way out in the event of an uncomfortable situation.

l. What time is an appropriate curfew?

> Even adults arrive home at a reasonable time in order to be able to meet the responsibilities of the following day. On weekends, midnight might be considered reasonable during the high school years with the occasional extension for special events such as prom. In fact, some states impose a midnight curfew on drivers during the first year of their license.

If you always keep in mind that you are a child of God, you will act like a child of God. If you always keep in mind that you are a tabernacle of God, you will always respect your body and that of others because you will know that He is within you. If you always keep in mind that you live within God Himself, you will know that His loving arms are around you to protect you and guide your steps. (2346-2347)

"Lord, be the guide of my thoughts, word, and actions." Always remember the power of a personal relationship with God and the Blessed Mother, their presence in your life, the power of prayer and the sacraments, especially Reconciliation and Eucharist.

Reflection: III. Spousal love is sacramental love

Marriage is a Sacrament

1. Marriage is both a private and public celebration. The couple confers the sacrament on each other, but they recite their vows at the nuptial Mass before the entire Body of Christ. The priest, who takes the place of Jesus, is the Church's witness to their union. Why is it important to the community for couples to announce their vows in public? (Its importance can be both practical and spiritual.) Can love ever be solely private between two people, both in the practical sense and in the spiritual sense? Authentic love, by its very nature, is centered on God and others.   In image of the Trinity, authentic love necessarily overflows as a continuous and active gift of self.   (1069, 1630-1632)

2. The marriage of Adam and Eve was the beginning of God's mission for mankind. The wedding feast at Cana was the beginning of Christ's redemptive mission. It was also the beginning of Mary's co-redemptive mission. Was it the beginning of a mission for the wedding couple? Is every wedding the beginning of a *new* mission? (372-373, 1603-1605, 1617)

3. Moses allowed divorce because the heart of man was hardened. Mankind had lost the sense of sin. The people of the Old Testament were at a disadvantage. They did not know Jesus, Who came to us as God's **Word** in the flesh. They did not know the Jesus Who suffered and died for our salvation. They did not know the Holy Spirit, Who is within us as our constant supplier of *grace*, which He gives bountifully in the Sacrament of Matrimony as a constant help to husband and wife. They had God's commandments and understood obedience to His *laws and to the prophets*. We have the guidance of the Church, the Body of Christ, in Whom we intimately live. We have the Eucharist, Christ intimately living within us. We have the advantage of so much more. (1601-1605, 1617)

    The people of the Old Testament knew about love, but they could not know about the kind of love that Jesus brought. What is special about His Love? How can we perpetuate it in our own lives? (1427, 1432, 1989)
    How does frequent reception of the Sacraments of Penance and Holy Eucharist sustain the vitality of Christ's love in us? (1264, 1394, 1426, 1436, 1863)

4. Is the love of husband and wife, expressed in intercourse, separate from the love shared with each other and with their children in the daily routines of life? Is it a separate event, or is the love they share through intercourse a love that encompasses all that they are and all that they give to their family and to others? (1641-1643, 1644, 2361, 2363, 2367, 2369)

Sacraments

5. "There, but for the grace of God, go I." We have so many reasons to say it. God gives us every grace we need, just for the asking. It doesn't mean that all the difficulties in life will go away. But, it *does* mean that He will be our **Partner** (for that is what grace is) through each and every trial. It *does* mean that He will be our **Partner** in every step of life that we take! We meet Jesus most intimately in His seven sacraments. Through reception of the sacraments, can you see His vital presence in every aspect of our lives? (Refer to page 43.) (1084, 1113, 1127, 1210, 1211, 1996-2005)

    Is it important to thank God frequently for these most generous gifts of Himself? (224, 1328, 2637)

Single Life

6. Is sexuality important for unmarried people? Of course! Being male or female is who we are as persons. It incorporates our entire being. Because they are not bound by the normal restrictions of family life, they are, in some respects, more free to love and serve others generously for God. They are in some ways more free to fulfill their roles of motherhood and fatherhood to all in the world. Can you think of some examples? Are there certain careers more suited than others to the fullness of generosity? How can anyone in any career fulfill this role of service to others? (2231, 2544-2550)

Religious Life

7.   Consecrated virginity is a very special call from God. Men and women who consecrate themselves to God forsake all others for Him alone. Filled with an undivided love for God, they are committed to spend their life solely for Him, in His service. They are spouses of God and the Church. They are mothers and fathers to God's people in the world, generously serving wherever they are called. There are great saints in heaven who have answered this higher call to holiness and are models for every man and woman on earth. Is there a particular priest or religious that you admire? What is his/her special way of bringing Christ to others? Is this person fulfilling a role of motherhood or fatherhood in the world? (914-927, 928-930-, 931-933, 2544-2550)

Refer back to page 51 to consider the gift of consecration that Joseph made. He had a tremendous love for Mary, surpassed only by his love for God.

Mary and Joseph were the first to be called to this kind of consecrated life for the sake of Jesus. They answered God's call without hesitation out of love for Him and all of us. God rewarded them with countless blessings for the sacrificial love they lived each day. In all the countless perplexing circumstances of their lives, they trusted in God's wisdom. They trusted Him while they waited for answers, and they trusted Him when there were no answers. Their roles serve as models for those who are called to be fathers and mothers to the world. (499-507, 1618-1620, 1812-1832)

Do you have a favorite saint? Can you think about the personal qualities of this saint? Do these qualities exemplify the fullness of masculinity or femininity? (922-924, 1618-1620, 1579)

A final question to think about: Does God need anyone? The answer is No. But, He **chooses to use us -- to build up His Kingdom**. As the Father sent the Son, the Son with the Holy Spirit sends us into the world to labor in His fields. He uses our hands, our legs, our eyes, our ears, our voices, and all that we are, to accomplish His work. As members of His Body, we live "through Him, with Him, and in Him." Let this be our constant prayer, "My Jesus, I love You. Help me to love others. Help me to love them for You."

BIBLIOGRAPHY

Several books have been written on each of the topics discussed. In the interest of simplicity, I tried to suggest books that are directly instructional in nature. I would especially recommend the first books listed which are rather complementary to this manuscript.

John Paul II *The Theology of the Body, Human Love in the Divine Plan,* Pauline Books and Media, 1997.

Evert, Jason *Theology of Her Body, Discovering the Beauty of Mystery of Femininity,* Ascension Press, 2009

Evert, Jason *Theology of His Body, Discovering the Strength and Mission of Masculinity,* Ascension Press, 2009

Percy, Anthony *The Theology of the Body Made Simple,* Pauline Books and Media, 2006.

West, Christopher *Theology of the Body for Beginners,* Ascension Press, 2004.

West, Christopher *Theology of the Body Explained,* Pauline Books and Media, 2003.

West, Christopher *Good News About Sex and Marriage,* Servant Books, 2000.

For Adolescent Instruction:

Hajduk, David *God's Plan for You, Life, Love, Marriage and Sex,* The Theology of the Body for Young People, Pauline Books and Media, 2006.

Kurey, Mary-Louise *Standing With Courage,* Our Sunday Visitor, 2002.

Pinto, Matthew and Evert, Jason
  Did Adam and Eve Have Belly Buttons? Ascension Press, 2003.

Pinto, Matthew and Evert, Jason *Did Jesus Have A Last Name?* Ascension Press, 2005.

Other Valuable Resources:

"Watch Me Grow" brochures from Little One Publishing, LLC., P.O. Box 4833, Baltimore, MD 21211 www.littleonepublishing.com

Aquilina, Mike. *Talking to Youth About Sexuality, A Parents' Guide,* Our Sunday Visitor, Inc., 1995.

Bonacci, Mary Beth, *Real Love,* Ignatius Press, 1996.

Cloud, Henry and Townsend, John. *Boundaries With Kids,* Zondervan, 1998.

Davies, Helen M. M.D. *Sex Instruction in the Home,* Real Press, 1993.

Dunn, Patrick M.D. *Educating In Chastity,* Human Life International, 1989.

Hahn, Scott *First Comes Love,* Doubleday, 2002

Hardon, John A. S.J. *The Catholic Family in the Modern World,* The Leaflet Missal Company, 1991.

Hardon, John A. S.J. *The Eucharist: Foundation of the Christian Family,* Eternal Life, 1992.

Kippley, John F. *Sex and the Marriage Covenant, A Basis for Morality,* The Couple to Couple League International., Inc., 1991.

Kippley, John F. *Marriage is For Keeps: Foundations for Christian Marriage,* The Foundation for the Family 1994.

Lovasik, Lawrence G. *The Catholic Family Handbook,* Sophia Institute Press, 2000.

Mast, Colleen Kelly. *Love and Life*, Ignatius Press, 1986.

Meeker, Dr. Meg *Strong Fathers Strong Daughters: Ten Secrets Every Father Should Know, Regnery Publishing, 2006*

Mother Mary Claudia. *The Little Church of the Family,* Arlington Catholic Herald, 1993.

Murphy, Ann and John. *Sex Education and Successful Parenting,* Pauline Books and Media, 1996.

Sattler, H. Vernon C.Ss.R. *Challenging Children to Chastity*, Central Bureau of the Catholic Verein of America, 1991.

Sheen, Bishop Fulton J., *The Divine Romance*, Alba House, New York, 2003

Sherrer, Catherine and Bernard. *The Joyful Mysteries of Life*, Family Publications, Ignatius Press, 1966.

Stenson, James B. *Preparing For Adolescence,* Scepter Booklets, 1990.

Stenson, James B. *Preparing For Peer Pressure,* Scepter Booklets, 1988.

Stenson, James B. *Upbringing, A Discussion Handbook for Parents of Young Children*, Scepter Publishers, Inc., 2004.

Welborn, Amy, "The Prove It" Series, Our Sunday Visitor, 2002.

Whitehead Margaret M. *Sex Education: The Catholic Scene*, Women For Faith and Family, *1993.*

Wolfe, Jaymie Stuart. The Call to Adoption, Becoming Your Child's Family, Pauline Books and Media, 2005.

The Couple to Couple League (ccli.org), *The Art of Natural Family Planning Student Guide*, 2nd edition, 2011.

The following Vatican documents may also be very useful:

Pontifical Council for the Family, *The Truth and Meaning of Human Sexuality*.

Pope John Paul II, *Letter to Families*

Pope John Paul II, *Familiaris Consortio*

Pope John Paul II, *Mulieris Dignitatem*

Pope John Paul II, *Redemptoris Mater*

Pope John Paul II, *Evangelium Vitae*, (The Gospel of Life)

Sacred Congregation for the Doctrine of the Faith, *Declaration on Certain Questions Concerning Sexual Ethics.*

Sacred Congregation for Catholic Education, *Educational Guidance in Human Love.*

ILLUSTRATIONS

Diagram A : Female Reproductive Organs

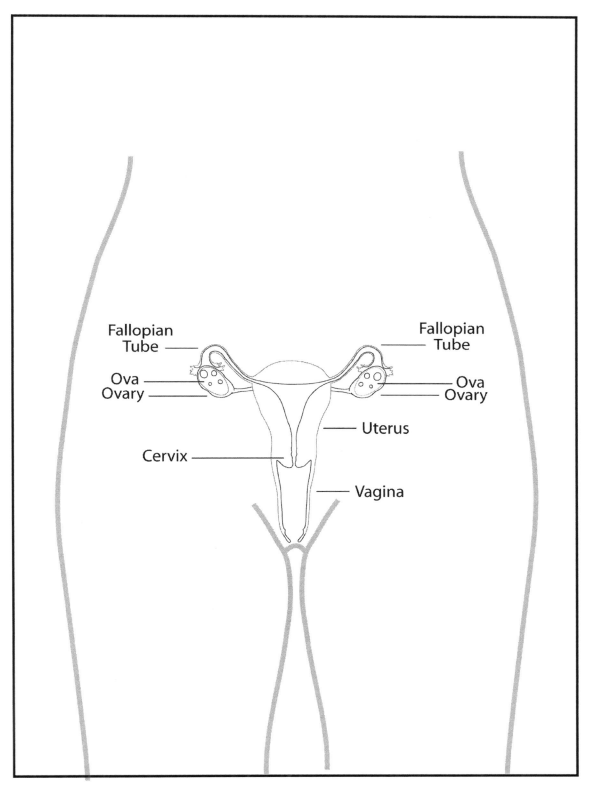

Fallopian Tube

Ova

Ovary

Cervix

Fallopian Tube

Ova

Ovary

Uterus

Vagina

Front View

Diagram B : Female Menstrual Cycle

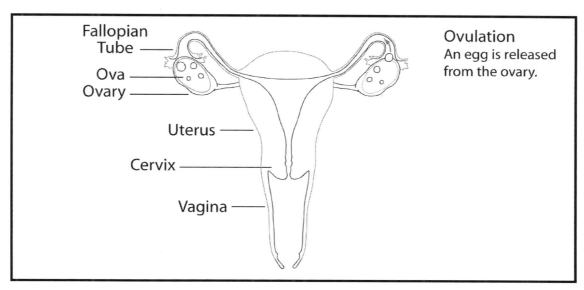

Fallopian Tube

Ova

Ovary

Uterus

Cervix

Vagina

Ovulation
An egg is released from the ovary.

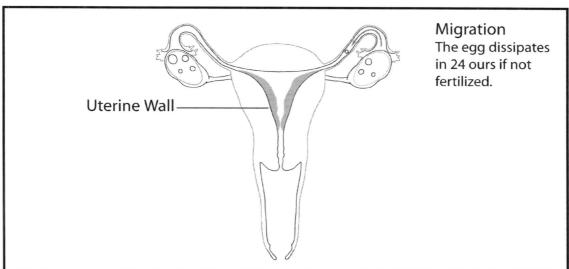

Uterine Wall

Migration
The egg dissipates in 24 ours if not fertilized.

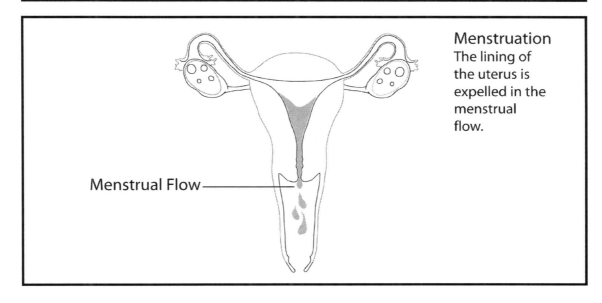

Menstrual Flow

Menstruation
The lining of the uterus is expelled in the menstrual flow.

Diagram C : Male Reproductive Organs

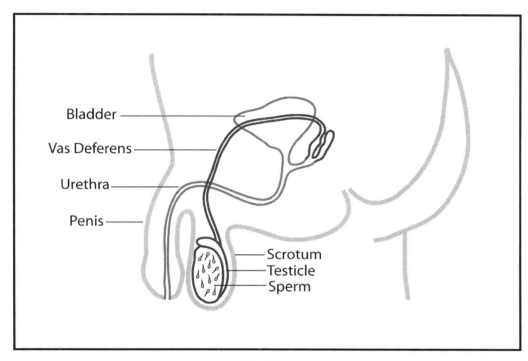

Bladder

Vas Deferens

Urethra

Penis

Scrotum
Testicle
Sperm

Side View

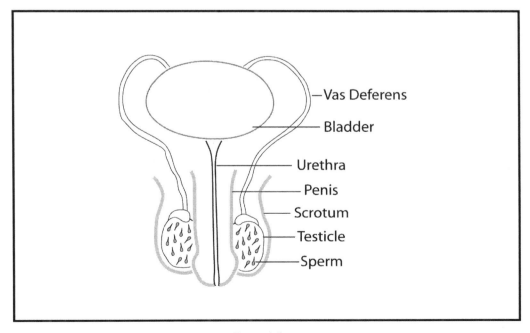

Vas Deferens

Bladder

Urethra

Penis

Scrotum

Testicle

Sperm

Front View

About the Author

Carolyn J. Smith has been married to her husband, Jim, for 42 years. She is the mother of eight daughters and two sons and the grandmother of 15 (and counting). She and her family live in Columbia, Maryland.

Carolyn homeschooled six of their children and was a member of TORCH, Traditions of Roman Catholic Homes. She taught Religious Education for 20 years, which included preparation for the sacraments of Penance and Eucharist and teamed with her husband for Confirmation Preparation. She is a volunteer counselor for a local pregnancy center. For many years, she and her husband acted as a sponsor couple in helping to prepare young couples for marriage.

She formed the Family Life curriculum at a private school in the Baltimore area and she taught this curriculum to girls in grades four through eight. Carolyn also served as a consultant on the Family Life Committee for two parishes in Baltimore. In her home parish, she used this book, *Growing Up in God's Image* (formerly titled *Family Love and Growing Up*) to guide parents through the discussion of the facts of life with their children. There were separate nights for the boys with their fathers and for the girls with their mothers. She has spoken on Sexuality at the NACHE (National Association of Catholic Home Educators) Conferences in Manassas, Virginia and at the Catholic Family Expo in Baltimore, Maryland as well as small groups of women in the Baltimore, Maryland area.

Made in the USA
Columbia, SC
11 August 2020